BEHIND THE VENEE

The South Shoreditch Furniture Trade and its Buildings

C000171815

Published by English Heritage, Kemble Drive, Swindon SN2 2GZ
www.english-heritage.org.uk
English Heritage is the Government's statutory adviser on all aspects of the historic environment.

© English Heritage 2006

Images (except as otherwise shown) © English Heritage.NMR
or © Crown copyright.NMR.

First published 2006

ISBN-10 1-873592-96-5
ISBN-13 978-1-873592-96-0
Product code 51204

British Library Cataloguing in Publication Data
A CIP catalogue record for this book is available from the British Library.

All rights reserved
No part of this publication may be reproduced or transmitted in any form or by any means, electronic
or mechanical, including photocopying, recording or any information or retrieval system, without the
permission in writing from the publisher.

Application for the reproduction of images should be made to the National Monuments Record. Every
effort has been made to trace the copyright holders and we apologise in advance for any unintentional
omissions, which we would be pleased to correct in any subsequent edition of this book.

The National Monuments Record is the public archive of English Heritage. For more information
contact NMR Enquiry and Research Services, National Monuments Record Centre, Kemble Drive,
Swindon SN2 2GZ; telephone 01793 414600.

Brought to publication by Joan Hodsdon, Publishing, English Heritage,
Kemble Drive, Swindon SN2 2GZ

Edited by John Button
Page layout by Bookcraft Ltd, Stroud, Gloucestershire
Printed in Belgium by Deckers Druk

BEHIND THE VENEER

The South Shoreditch Furniture Trade and its Buildings

Joanna Smith and Ray Rogers

Contents

Frontispiece *An aerial view of South Shoreditch in 2002, showing the mixture of Victorian and Edwardian buildings, post-war additions and large-scale late 20th-century redevelopment.*

Acknowledgements

This book is derived from a survey carried out by Joanna Smith and Tara Draper-Stumm. The graphics were produced by Andrew Donald and the photography was by Derek Kendall. Other help, in various forms, was provided by Susie Barson, Jonathan Clarke, Emily Gee, Colum Giles, Peter Guillery, Paddy Pugh, Treve Rosoman, Mike Seaforth, Charles Walker and June Warrington.

The assistance of the following individuals and organisations is gratefully acknowledged: David Dewing and his colleagues at the Geffrye Museum, the staff of Hackney Archives Department and London Metropolitan Archives, Edmond Harbour of HDG Ltd, Oliver Lebus, Rapid Eye, SCP, Urban Practitioners and James Yorke at the Victoria and Albert Museum. We would like to thank all those who gave us access to their properties or supplied us with information.

Foreword

South Shoreditch is a compact district that lies immediately to the north of the City of London. This close proximity has shaped its historical development and will undoubtedly continue to exert an influence on its future. Today the area lies at the centre of a band that has become known in development contexts as the 'City fringe', identified by the Greater London Authority as a strategic zone earmarked for considerable change. One of the most acute sites of development pressure is South Shoreditch. But this is also an area of considerable historical interest, with a richly varied and visually compelling architectural legacy of Victorian and Edwardian commercial buildings. Much of the inheritance derives from the area having been a major centre of the furniture trade from the mid-19th century to the mid-20th century.

The management of change in the City fringe is a major public policy issue for Londoners. Using South Shoreditch as a model, English Heritage, in partnership with the London Borough of Hackney and the Greater London Authority, has been exploring ways to manage future development in the City fringe through a co-ordinated planning approach. In addition, English Heritage has undertaken a comprehensive appraisal of the historic character and significance of South Shoreditch and its distinctive and predominant buildings types. It is partly from the resulting study that this publication is drawn.

This book therefore serves to highlight the architectural history of the area and the conservation and planning issues associated with it. It also underscores the necessity of proper historical evaluation when attempting to understand the character of an area.

Sir Neil Cossons
Chairman, English Heritage

> '... the industrial activity of London shows no sign of abatement. Individuals and individual trades may suffer, but her vitality and productive energy, stimulated by a variety of resources probably unequalled in their number and extent by those of any other city ancient or modern, remain unimpaired. London is supreme not only in variety, but in total magnitude.'
>
> Charles Booth, *Life and Labour of the People in London*, 1902, vol 5

1
INTRODUCTION

The importance of South Shoreditch to the English furniture industry was twofold: as a centre of production and as its commercial heart. This dual significance was typical of London; in the capital, making and selling mattered equally and, as a result, it had an economy as 'diverse, robust and productive as that of many European nations'.[1] In 1851 the number of Londoners involved in manufacturing was almost equal to the entire population of Liverpool, England's second largest city, added to which there were unparalleled numbers in the service sector.[2] The range of industries was wide and none predominated, as the metal trades did in Sheffield, or textiles in Manchester, although the capital had nationally important concentrations of printing and tanning. From an enormously diverse base, the trend in the 18th and 19th centuries was towards specialisation in finished goods such as clothing or coach making, the metropolis invariably leading the way in setting fashions and shaping the nation's tastes.

The London trades had a complex geography. Some, like tanning or hatmaking, were concentrated in specific areas; others such as building and engineering were more widely distributed. From the 18th century a manufacturing belt edged the capital's historic core – the City of London – to the north, east and south. During the 19th century some of London's trades, such as silk weaving and shipbuilding, declined into insignificance, while others like electrical engineering and food processing emerged. Between the 1850s and the 1950s many of the capital's trades went through unprecedented change, adapting to the emergence of new markets at home and abroad, new technologies and production methods, and developments

New and old furniture in the factory of J Wernick (Furniture) Ltd, 16 Provost Street.

Fig 1 *Making and selling embodied in the firm of B Cohen & Sons, whose factories and showrooms dominated the southern end of Curtain Road from the 1880s until the 1940s. (Geffrye Museum, London)*

Fig 2 (opposite) *Surviving warehouses and showrooms on Tabernacle Street and Clere Street. Commercial rebuilding had started here by the 1870s, but the taller of these buildings postdate a fire of 1894.*

in distribution, marketing and sales. The consequences of these changes were felt across the spectrum of commercial activity in London, which broadly divided into a retail market in the West End and a wholesale market in the City and East End.

During the first half of the 20th century new manufacturing districts were developed on the outskirts of the capital, but some of the older industrial quarters persisted. After the 1960s manufacturing in London went into steep decline, and many of its industrial sites were redeveloped. Today South Shoreditch is amongst the best preserved of the Victorian manufacturing districts (Fig 2), retaining a distinctive urban landscape that was largely shaped by its dominant trade.

Historically London was the principle centre of the English furniture trade, famed in the 18th century for makers such as George Hepplewhite and Thomas Chippendale. The perception of furniture making in the Georgian period is as more of a craft than an industry, with skilled artisans employed in workshops producing bespoke high-quality goods for an aristocratic and burgeoning middle-class market. In reality the trade was already moving away from its craft origins, with some production of ready-made furniture and an increasingly complex manufacturing and retail structure. At the end of the 18th century the showrooms, workshops and – more rarely – factories of the trade were primarily concentrated in the City of London and the West End, though some production was already taking place in the eastern districts. It was the emergence of a mass market for lower-priced ready-made goods during the 19th century that brought the East End furniture trade to pre-eminence.

The emergence of a mass market did not lead initially to large-scale factory production within the furniture industry. Rising demand was met by a proliferation of highly competitive small-scale manufacturers, and by outworking in the home. Mechanisation and new production methods did have an impact and a few large factories were built, but the character of the trade favoured a more diverse approach to manufacturing. This was partly because furniture came in a huge range of shapes, sizes and styles, too broad for easy standardisation, and was subject to fluctuations in demand that made large production runs uneconomic. A smaller scale of manufacturing was more flexible and responsive, able to adapt to changing fashions and novel forms (Fig 3).

The production process was broken down into a number of stages carried out by different businesses in close proximity to one another, so that, as Peter Hall observed, the real assembly line ran through the streets.[3] This required the presence of a host of ancillary trades, supplying the raw materials, finishes, accessories, tools and machinery required in the production process. The result was a district that functioned as a sort of giant dispersed factory and showroom for the trade.

The transformation of South Shoreditch into a specialised commercial and industrial quarter occurred over the last quarter of the 19th century (Fig 4). The furniture trade required different types of facility – for manufacturing, storage and distribution. There were also competing demands from other commercial activities, as the district had important printing, tobacco, boot and shoe industries. Furthermore, a significant residential population had to be accommodated and space

Fig 3 *Two display cabinets, the lower in the form of a credenza, for the drawing room. This eclectically styled furniture was intended for the better end of the ready-made market, designed for the best rooms of the house. The illustration is taken from the 1880 catalogue of C & R Light. Such publications were one of the ways that the East End trade advertised its wares. (Geffrye Museum, London)*

Fig 4 *Former workshops of the 1870s and 1880s on Luke Street and Phipp Street, built primarily for the furniture trade. Close to the main thoroughfares, these manufacturing spaces were used by many kinds of businesses including small-scale manufacturers and wholesalers with showrooms nearby.*

found for new institutional and civic facilities, such as schools, churches, council buildings, police stations, fire stations and law courts. The result was a pattern of mercantile boulevards lined by commercial warehouses and industrial side streets of workshops and small factories forming concentrated quarters for manufacturing. Intermixed with these were public buildings, tenement blocks and timber yards.

Much of this distinctive townscape, grafted onto the older footprint of an already developed City suburb, survived redevelopment in the 20th century (Frontispiece). The area suffered some damage in the Second World War and several large-scale commercial buildings have been erected on bomb-damaged sites. The furniture trade, long in decline, finally collapsed in the 1980s. Now the once-dominant industry of South Shoreditch has gone, but significant numbers of its buildings have remained to find alternative uses and a new vibrancy in the early 21st century.

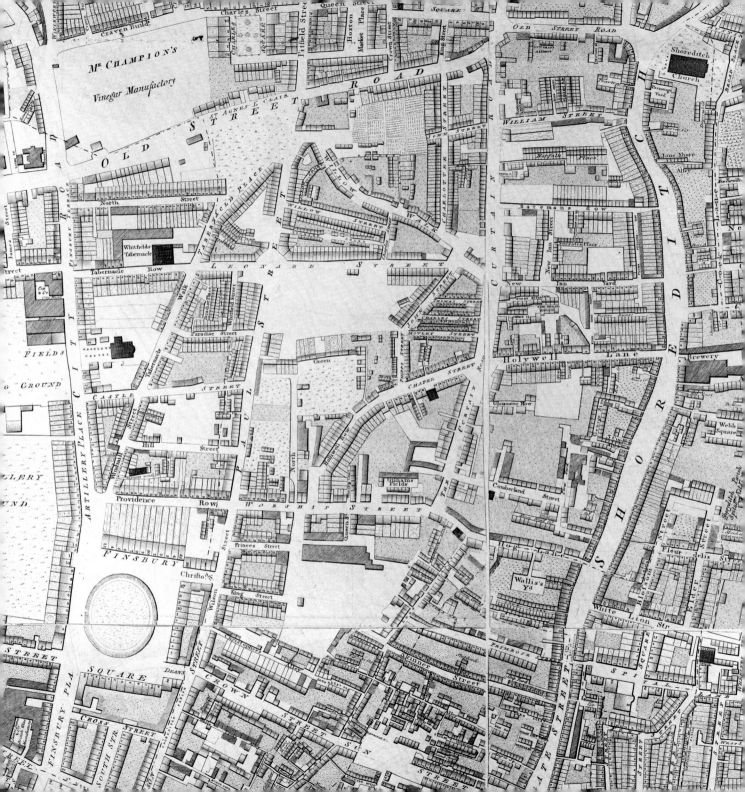

'It is an industrial suburb, inhabited by workers at small trades, and is full of tenement houses. It has been characterised as "the city of smaller industries and the lesser ingenuities".'

Walter Besant, *London North of the Thames*, 1911

2

THE EVOLUTION OF AN INDUSTRIAL QUARTER

Richard Horwood's map of London, published in 1799, shows South Shoreditch at a key point in its development (Fig 5). Fifty years earlier large areas of open land remained between the main commercial arteries – Shoreditch High Street which linked the City of London with the original settlement around the parish church, Curtain Road, Old Street and the City Road. This growth had been shaped by proximity to the City and a fragmented pattern of development.

From the 1770s new roads were laid out, some like Paul Street and Leonard Street to a coherent plan, others such as Holywell Row and Rivington Street in a more ad hoc and piecemeal fashion. These were lined by terraces of generally small brick houses, producing a street pattern that remains today. By the end of the 18th century South Shoreditch was a thriving residential, manufacturing and commercial City suburb. Its main thoroughfares contained shops and dwellings occupied by artisans and tradesmen serving the City and the local population. Interspersed with these were public houses, livery stables and timber yards, and a scattering of industrial premises such as dye houses and coach-makers' workshops. There was also some silk-weaving overspill from its principal centre in the adjacent districts of Spitalfields and Bethnal Green, usually based in houses that combined domestic and industrial use.

In the early part of the 19th century the character of South Shoreditch, and of the wider City fringe of which it formed part, began to change. Industrial and commercial use intensified, and shops and businesses increasingly began to cater for wholesale and specialist markets. As a result some houses in South Shoreditch were replaced or converted, and many back yards and gardens were built over with workshops. Some piecemeal commercial redevelopment occurred on the main streets – Curtain Road, City Road and Old Street – but many existing buildings were adapted to new uses. In 1857 the neighbourhood

Fig 5 *South Shoreditch in 1799, straddling four sheets of Richard Horwood's map. Much of the development west of the City Road area was then recent; the extensive ribbon development along Shoreditch High Street and on the City borders to the south was older.*

was described in *The Builder* as having a 'picturesque' appearance
(Fig 6). Any lingering residential gentility was now in retreat as the
population of the parish of Shoreditch swelled from around 35,000 in
1801 to 69,000 in 1831, peaking around 1861 at 129,364. Much of this
growth was absorbed by the two northerly sub-districts of the parish,
Hoxton and Haggerston, but South Shoreditch also had its share of
poorly built cottages, back alley dwellings and tenement conversions.

The industries that congregated on the City's periphery during the
19th century were often secondary or service trades, such as printing,
building, footwear, transport, food processing and pharmacy. By the
end of the 19th century these manufacturing areas typically contained
a mixture of industries deriving mutual benefit from close proximity,
providing work for one another or having equipment such as sewing
machines or raw materials like leather in common. Certain trades
came to dominate particular localities. In the East End, Shoreditch
became noted principally for furniture, and Whitechapel for clothing.
All benefited from an abundant labour force, many of whom were
prepared to work in the 'dishonourable' sector of these trades – the
non-unionised, poorly paid, and less skilled segment. This led to their
castigation as 'sweated' industries, characterised by high levels of
exploitation and impoverishment. However, a degree of craft-based
skill continued as did aspects of artisan working. For example, furniture
makers continued to own their tools well into the era of factory
production. Often generations of families worked at the same trade, but
the workforce was constantly replenished by high levels of immigration.
From the 1880s this included a large number of East European Jews,
who made a significant contribution to the furniture and clothing trades
at all levels from worker to proprietor.

Another factor in the rise of the East End trades was proximity to their
markets, especially important for industries producing consumer goods
such as footwear, furniture and clothing. The capital itself comprised the
single largest and most concentrated market for these goods. Between
1851 and 1939 the metropolitan population rose from 2.6m to 8.6m, and
many thousands of new dwellings were erected, creating a huge demand for
domestic goods. Furthermore, as London lay at the centre of the country's

Fig 6 *336 Old Street, photographed in 1910.
These modest commercial premises were rebuilt
around 1880 but the old wooden shop sign had been
present since at least the 1850s, presumably intended
as an advertisement for the occupants, a firm of
shop fitters. (Corporation of London, London
Metropolitan Archives)*

Fig 7 *The canalside factory of American manufacturer Henry Herrmann in Dod Street, Limehouse, in 1891. The imported wood was brought by barge from the docks, and an electric crane lifted it into the timber yard. On the far side of the canal another yard is identifiable by its stacks of timber and seasoning sheds.*

transport network, manufacturers and distributors were easily able to access regional markets and the international trade.

The capital's transport infrastructure underwent a revolution during the 19th century, and many new schemes had a direct impact on the development of the eastern districts. One of the earliest was the opening in 1820 of the Regent's Canal, linking the Paddington arm of the Grand Junction Canal in the west of London with the River Thames at Limehouse, passing to the north of Shoreditch. The canal provided a direct connection to the growing network of enclosed docks and riverside wharves, bringing imported raw materials and manufactured goods and export facilities within easy reach of the East End trades (Fig 7). The railways came in 1840 with the opening of the terminus of the Eastern Counties Railway on Shoreditch High Street, converted in 1881 into Bishopsgate Goods Station after the opening of another terminus at Liverpool Street to the south. The North London Line followed in 1861–5, the construction of its viaduct cutting a swathe through the eastern half of South Shoreditch. Metropolitan

Fig 8 *10 Great Eastern Street was built in 1879. Its wedge-shaped site was the result of having cut the new road across an existing street pattern. Behind passes the disused viaduct of the North London Line while beyond lies the remains of the Bishopsgate Goods Station.*

Fig 9 *C & R Light was one of the best known Shoreditch wholesale furniture dealers and manufacturers. Their substantial showrooms at 134–146 Curtain Road were built between 1881 and 1887 to the designs of Richard Crease Hamilton. The building still dominates the northern end of the street; the firm moved out in 1918, since when it has had a variety of uses and occupants.*

road improvements during the 1870s also had an impact. A major new thoroughfare, Great Eastern Street, was cut diagonally through the area in 1876 (Fig 8). This was designed to improve communications between the east and west of London by linking Commercial Street, another metropolitan street improvement, with Old Street. At the same time other roads, including the northern end of Shoreditch High Street, were widened.

These works brought great upheaval to the local population and businesses. They also brought great commercial opportunities as the new roads were built up with large-scale premises (Fig 9), transforming 'dirty little streets into noble urban highways, lined by splendid shops, spacious warehouses, and the veritable palaces of modern trade'.[4] This encouraged a building boom across the district that lasted from the 1870s until after 1900.

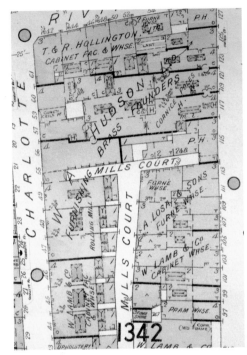

Fig 10 *An example of commercial densification and back lands development. In the 1870s and 1880s the houses on, and yard buildings between, Curtain Road and Charlotte Road and around Mills Court were replaced by showroom-warehouses and workshops. By the 1920s, when this Goad Insurance map was produced, four businesses – including the cabinet ironmongers and furnishing brass founders, W A Hudson – occupied almost all of the buildings.*

Fig 11 *A view of Curtain Road looking north from the junction with Great Eastern Street taken around 1900. The carts and barrows were used to transport the semi-finished furniture back and forth between the makers and the wholesale dealers. (Hackney Archives Department)*

By the early 20th century South Shoreditch had a dense urban landscape with a highly mixed building stock, often perpetuating older layouts and property boundaries (Fig 10). A similar pattern of development existed in the other manufacturing districts of the capital, such as Clerkenwell and Bermondsey, but there was also strong local distinctiveness, as Charles Booth observed in the 1880s in describing the East End:

> Each district has its character – its peculiar flavour. One seems to be conscious of it in the streets. It may be in the faces of the people, or in what they carry – perhaps a reflection is thrown in this way from the prevailing trades – or it may lie in the sounds one hears, or in the character of the buildings.[5]

The distinctiveness of South Shoreditch came primarily from the daily business of making, moving and displaying the products of the furniture trade (Fig 11). The endurance of the industry here enabled the area to retain its character as a specialised industrial quarter through much of the 20th century, and ensured the survival of many of its Victorian and Edwardian warehouses, workshops and factories.

'What is the real character of East End furniture? Is it good, bad or indifferent? Now, we can make no more conclusive reply to this inquiry than to say, that East End furniture is anything to order.'

Cabinet and Upholstery Advertiser, 13 October 1877, 7

3
THE EAST END FURNITURE TRADE

The heyday of the East End furniture trade was from 1860 to 1945, when it was at the forefront of new developments in design, marketing and manufacturing. The furniture district was centred in South Shoreditch, spreading across several adjoining areas including Bethnal Green and Hoxton. The first makers were documented in the area in the mid- to late 18th century, and chair manufactories on City Road and Curtain Road were noted in trade directories of the 1790s. Lone artisan makers occupying houses and rear workshops were present on Charlotte Road in the 1830s and probably earlier (Fig 12). Such enterprises probably supplied dealers in the City as well as local outlets, including a furniture warehouse and showroom at the corner of Curtain Road and Old Street.

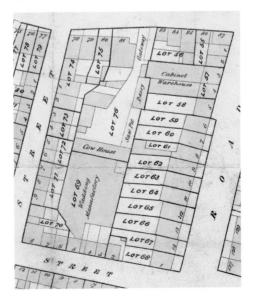

Fig 12 *This sales particular map of 1832 gives an indication of furniture-making activity at that date. Lot 76 includes a sawpit, probably used by the cabinet maker Thomas Pizzey who occupied the front house, 81 Old Street. South is the wadding manufactory of Messrs Hempstead and Co, probably supplying the upholsterers of the district, while lot 57, 3–5 Curtain Road, comprises the cabinet warehouse and showroom of Messrs Brown. (Hackney Archives Department)*

A collection of cutting blades at 16 Provost Street (opposite).

which are used for chair-work and morticing are particularly clever, because all the marking is automatic. Take, for instance, the back feet of a chair. Instead of marking after the old and somewhat uncertain method, the two pieces of wood are dropped into a shape or mould made for the purpose, and the boring bit pierces the wood in the right place, without any possible deviation. We need hardly say that this affords a perfect guarantee for *square* work; and,

work as incising, fluting, sunk panelling and moulding, and, indeed, any decoration which is required to be below the surface of the material. It is adjustable to any thickness of

Thicknessing and Moulding.

Turning.

moreover, it saves a great deal of time and skilled labour. Another machine of a similar character, attached to the same bench, is the one which cuts the tenons at a single operation. Our illustration of this process may explain the method. The cutter is armed with teeth as well as with a sort of revolving plane iron. The teeth cut the shoulder to the right depth, while the plane removes the superfluous wood.

wood, and is capable of producing any patterns. Looking at it as a mere fluting machine—the flutes it produces are always quite true and can, if required, be tapered. This machine, in conjunction with the carvers' benches, occupies an important position in the decorative section of the establishment. A room has been wisely set apart for " papering up," and the revolving drum which is now commonly used for this purpose

Band Sawing.

Fret Cutting.

Several other special appliances upon this ground floor might call for remark. We must, however, devote the limited space which remains at our disposal to a notice of the important operations which are performed on the floors above.

The principal piece of mechanism upon the next floor is the very useful carving and incising machine which is somewhat fully illustrated over-leaf. It is able to execute all such

is duly figured on the next page. It is upon this floor that the cabinet makers and others who receive the wood from the machines are busily employed in putting the various pieces together, and in doing that portion of the work which the " iron hand " cannot, as yet, perform. Our notice has more to do with the mechanism than the men and so we must pass over the better known processes of handwork which are

Fig 13 *These depictions of wood-working machinery and their operators are illustrated in an article in the* Cabinet Maker and Art Furnisher *in 1884. They indicate the range of machinery that had just been installed in the new steam cabinet and chair works of Morrison and Austin at the rear of 85 Worship Street.*

Fig 14 (opposite) *The impressive mid-19th-century showrooms of Moore and Hunton, furniture wholesalers, at 2–4 Paul Street and 53–65 Worship Street. The names of colonial centres where the firm did business once adorned the first-floor windows, lettered in gold.*

Mechanisation began to have an impact on the processing of timber from the 1840s, as steam saw-mills took over from hand sawing in pits. The introduction of powered machinery also affected another section of the timber trade, veneer cutting. Such technological advances lowered the cost of raw materials and encouraged the production of cheaper veneered furniture, where a thin slice of more valuable wood was applied to a carcass of less expensive timber.

As the market for cheaper goods grew, the East End makers and dealers came to the fore, encouraged by the emergence in the mid-19th century of West End furniture emporia like Maples, who bought in much of their stock. Some of the wholesalers had originated in the City of London and migrated to South Shoreditch in the 1860s and 1870s, driven out by rising rents and road and rail developments or lured north by the growing importance of the district. Other firms had local origins, emerging directly from the established furniture-making industry in the area. The sharp operating practices of these dealers, forcing the makers to outproduce and undersell one another, earned their businesses the epithet of 'slaughter houses' in the mid-19th century. By the 1880s Curtain Road and Great Eastern Street had become the principal wholesale market of the national trade.

At the same time furniture manufacturing began to partially mechanise, with the introduction of circular saws, joint cutters, planing and carving machines (Fig 13). Mills and machine shops appeared in South Shoreditch in the 1870s, but until the 1890s these were generally limited to the larger firms. Mechanisation of aspects of the production process contributed to lower prices, it being said in the 1890s that it was 'possible, almost, to purchase a suite for the sum that would have been demanded for a single article in the showrooms of our fathers'.[6]

In the late 19th century East End furniture was popularly associated with the cheap and nasty, often dismissed as 'Curtain Road stuff'. In reality all classes of work were made here, varying from 'the richly inlaid cabinet that may be sold for £100, or the carved chair that can be made to pass as rare "antique" workmanship, down to the gipsy tables that the maker sells for 9s a dozen, or ... cheap bedroom suites'.[7]

Fig 15 *Female and male workers in the upholstery shop of Harris Lebus on Paradise Place (later Clere Place) in c1900. (Courtesy of Oliver Lebus)*

The goods being made and sold in the district supplied a global market and included almost every conceivable item (Fig 14). These ranged from suites of furniture for drawing, dining and bedrooms to one-off items such as bookcases, cabinets, framed pictures and other decorative objects. The so-called 'comprehensive' dealers also supplied related furnishings, such as wallpapers, carpets, floor coverings and light shades. Everything came in a range of traditional and reproduction styles, from accurate replicas to items with a 'period flavour', as well as more contemporary treatments such as Arts and Crafts and, later, art deco. There was also a burgeoning demand for office furniture resulting from the growth of service industries and the government sector, and from associated office building.

The overseas market was important in encouraging innovations such as folding furniture, an early form of flat-packed products intended for assembly overseas. In 1895 William Henry Vaughan patented an entire suite of bedroom furniture, including a wardrobe, armchairs and a bed that could be folded into a 6ft case. The export trade was the particular preserve of the East End industry, facilitated by the area's access to the docks. This was largely directed towards the imperial colonies like Australia and South Africa, but there was also a significant market for British furniture in Europe, particularly in Germany, France and Belgium. Conversely, foreign manufacturers wanting to sell in the British market and regional makers looking to the London trade took showrooms in South Shoreditch, selling bentwood chairs from Austria, roll-top desks from the USA, chairs from High Wycombe and iron bedsteads from the Midlands.

The East End furniture industry retained the traditional craft divisions of the trade. Generally known as cabinet making, it comprised many subcategories, such as fancy cabinet, chair or sofa making. All in turn might use the services of specialists such as wood turners and cabinet carvers, who produced the more worked elements of the furniture. Finishing was divided between upholsterers, who did the 'soft work' of covering and stuffing, and french polishing. These were the only areas of significant employment for women in what was otherwise a male-dominated industry (Fig 15).

Rapid turnover of businesses was a characteristic trait of the furniture industry. Many small firms had short lives in shared or sublet premises, encouraged by relatively low start-up costs and a reliance on subcontracting. Bigger concerns moved around the district with great frequency, sometimes occupying a number of premises, expanding and contracting as the market dictated. Some moves were prompted by the lure of new premises, others by the frequent incidence of fire. Large companies were rare, but family-run businesses were common as were firms set up by ex-employees. This produced a tightly knit community, reinforced by close commercial relationships and mutual dependencies and sustained by the specialised quarter in which it operated.

Fig 16 *When 9–11 New Inn Street were photographed in 1907 all of these buildings were occupied by cabinet makers. A French polisher peers from the doorway of 9, while some chairs, finished and in skeletal form, stand on the pavement; such colonisation of the public areas for temporary storage was commonplace. (Corporation of London, London Metropolitan Archives)*

The trade's monopolisation of the area incorporated its streets and pavements, required for the movement and temporary storage of the pieces of furniture as they moved back and forth between the makers, wholesalers, upholsterers, polishers and buyers (Fig 16). Forecourts and archways were sometimes pressed into service as finishing spaces, and the noises and smells of the trade permeated the district.

> In Curtain Road, from Old Street to Great Eastern Street, at one time every shop save four was a wholesale furniture warehouse. Into Great Eastern Street, Rivington Street, Worship Street, City Road, Old Street, Scrutton Street, Tabernacle Street and all the intervening streets of that district wholesale furniture emporiums seemed to have been spilled. At any time during the week from the purlieus of Hoxton, from Old Ford, Bethnal Green, and the byways of Shoreditch could be seen vans and weird piles of furniture in unpolished or skeleton forms, … frames piled to a dizzy height on one barrow, two or three telescope dining-tables on another.[8]

The power of the wholesalers went into decline in the early 20th century as department, co-operative and multiple stores preferred to buy directly from the producers rather than through middlemen. After the First World War the area retained its importance as a manufacturing centre, but its innovatory role diminished. When factory based, assembly line production developed in the 1920s and 1930s it was based in outer London, not in Shoreditch or Bethnal Green. The working culture of the East End furniture district remained remarkably unchanged, rooted in the workshop and small factory, in specialised skills and craft divisions, and a tradition of hand making assisted by machinery.

SOUTH SHOREDITCH
FURNITURE AND FURNISHING TRADES:
BUILDING USE IN 1918

SHOWROOM - WAREHOUSES		FACTORIES AND WORKSHOPS
ASSOCIATED TRADES: VARNISH AND UPHOLSTERY SUPPLIERS, CABINET IRONMONGERS ETC.		TIMBER YARDS, TIMBER MERCHANTS, SAWMILLS AND WOOD - WORKING PREMISES

50   0   50   100   150   200   250 metres
50   0   50   100   150   200   250 yards

4
THE BUILDINGS OF THE EAST END FURNITURE TRADE

The types of buildings used by the furniture trade fall broadly into three categories: showroom-warehouses for displaying and storing goods; workspaces – workshops and factories for manufacturing; and associated timber yards and saw-mills supplying the raw materials. There was little constructional difference between the showroom-warehouses and the workshops and small factories, as all were designed as 'loose-fit' buildings with open floors and undefined spaces. They shared a standard vocabulary of architectural forms, yet there is a subtle hierarchy. The taller and more imposing premises were mainly used by the dealers and specialist suppliers, while manufacturing buildings were generally lower and functional in appearance. The timber yards had more specialised structures for storing and processing their products. What gave South Shoreditch its distinctive form was the close proximity and physical relationship between these different types of premises, which in combination enabled the furniture trade to flourish in the area (Fig 18).

Fig 17 (opposite) *A map of building use in South Shoreditch in 1918 showing the concentration of furniture-related activities and how these were intermixed.*

Fig 18 *The mixed commercial building stock of Leonard Street: a handsome showroom-warehouse of 1893 initially used by a firm of woodwork machinery dealers and, beyond, warehouses and workshops of the 1860s and 1870s used by furniture makers.*

The showroom-warehouse

The market is made and extended by the wholesale dealers in many ways; especially by providing show-rooms, by sending out representatives, by establishing agencies, by circulating catalogues (sometimes elaborate volumes) and price lists; and, perhaps to these should be added, by giving longer credit than the maker can usually afford. This is the wholesale dealer's chief function – the making of the market; and on its importance it is unnecessary to enlarge.

Ernest Aves, 'The furniture trade', 1889

The buildings used by the furniture wholesalers were essentially commercial warehouses. Almost all of the extant examples in South Shoreditch date from the period between 1870 and 1910. Most were built on a generous scale, ranging in height from three to five storeys over basements, with plain brick frontages of solid respectability. Inside a variety of functions had to be accommodated, and the main requirements of the users were for well-lit undivided floor space, loading and unloading facilities and, if possible, some means of moving the goods around the building.

Showroom-warehouses began to be built in the 1840s or 1850s and in appearance had much in common with their predecessors, the combined shop and dwelling (Fig 19). The main differences were those of scale – the showroom-warehouse generally being larger – and of function – upper floors being given over to commercial rather than domestic use.

Initially showroom-warehouses were built in a piecemeal fashion, but this changed with the metropolitan street improvements of the 1870s. Over the following decade an abundance of large-scale showroom-warehouses, sometimes grouped in vast monolithic blocks, were built along Great Eastern Street, Appold Street, and the north-west end of Shoreditch High Street. Even this amount of new building was insufficient to satisfy demand, so other streets, most notably Charlotte Road and Tabernacle Street, were transformed in the 1880s and

Fig 19 *William Bailey's trade card of c1870 depicts their newly built showroom-warehouse on Curtain Road. This building remained firmly in the tradition of a combined shop-and-dwelling, with a domestic appearance to the upper floors. (Hackney Archives Department)*

Fig 20 (opposite) *The transition of Charlotte Road from residential street to place of manufacture accelerated from the 1870s. Its workshops and warehouses are much taller and deeper than the buildings they replaced.*

Fig 21 *13–19 Curtain Road, built in 1861 for J B Richards, is one of the earliest examples of a fully developed showroom-warehouse. In 1881 the building became the showrooms and offices of B Cohen and Sons, one of the leading wholesale manufacturers and exporters in the district.*

Fig 22 *One of the largest speculative developments on Great Eastern Street, 76–82, built for Charles Bryant and William King between 1882 and 1884. Such lofty buildings, sometimes more impressive in scale than in detail, line the main roads of the district while the side-street premises are generally lower in height.*

1890s. Here the replacement of smaller-scale warehouses and Georgian houses with lofty four- or five-storey buildings produced a canyon-like streetscape (Fig 20). At the same time established businesses on Curtain Road and Old Street, eager to remain competitive, rebuilt, altered and enlarged their premises. This building boom had peaked by 1910 and only a few showroom-warehouses were built after this, one of the last being 50–52 Paul Street, erected as late as the 1950s or 1960s.

The earliest surviving example of a showroom-warehouse in its mature form is 13–19 Curtain Road, built as manufactory and showrooms for James Boswell Richards in 1861 (Fig 21). The façade of the building has all the standard elements, such as brick pilasters treated as a Giant Order and abundant glazing. The desire for more light led to a greater proportion of the elevation being used for windows than had hitherto been the case, and in many examples windows were paired or grouped with intermediate cast-iron colonnettes or mullions of brick or stone. From the 1890s the window lintels were often of wrought iron or steel spanning the space between the piers to optimise the openings. This stripped-down treatment limited the scope for decoration, and the elevations of these buildings often had to rely on scale and repetition of features for effect (Fig 22). Ornament was generally restricted to classical details such as moulded cornices, parapets and keystones over windows, or decorative flourishes like terracotta panels or bands of stone or stucco dressings. Because these buildings were for the wholesale rather than the retail trade and subject to frequent changes of occupant, more overt displays of external extravagance were probably deemed an unnecessary expense. A few firms, however, were not content with putting up 'the plain, square, stereotyped warehouse sort of thing',[9] preferring something more distinctive, such as the eclectically styled building at 125–130 Shoreditch High Street (Fig 23).

The scale of speculative development was another factor in the limited architectural vocabulary of showroom-warehouses. A handful of developers and builders were responsible for a significant proportion

Fig 23 *The striking showroom-warehouse, 125–130 Shoreditch High Street, viewed from the graveyard of St Leonard's Church. This variation on the usual theme was built in 1877 for Edward Wells & Co, cabinet ironmongers, to the designs of Fowler and Hill. Its showrooms were originally used to display stoves, ranges, gas fittings and other manufactured brass items.*

Fig 24 86–90 Curtain Road, a speculative development of four showroom-warehouses by local furniture manufacturer Edward Gates, was built in c1892. By the 1930s one business, A Oakden and Sons, occupied the entire group. This plan shows the buildings before refurbishment in 2003–4 and includes later alterations such as party-wall openings and inserted goods lifts.

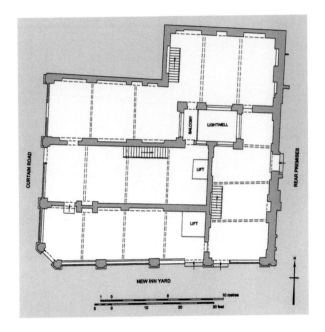

of the buildings, the most prolific being Charles Bryant and the King family. William Isaac and Edwin Franklin King built several near-identical blocks, including 54–62, 75–79 and 76–82 Great Eastern Street. Such men rarely employed architects and built to a no-frills formula (Fig 24). Some owner-occupiers or small-scale developers did use architects, usually drawn from the workaday ranks of the profession. Competent practitioners with commercial practices, these included James William Brooker, who in 1877 designed the imposing building at 40–42 Great Eastern Street as a speculation for the cabinet ironmonger Edward Wells and Company (Fig 58).

The internal arrangements of the showroom-warehouse generally followed a similar pattern. The basement was often used for packing the finished goods into crates, and therefore tended to be raised slightly above ground level to allow light and air to reach the interior, and for ease of access. Above this were up to three floors of showrooms. These were generally uninterrupted spaces, with functional cast-iron columns

Fig 25 *The showrooms of Harris Lebus at 62–72 Tabernacle Street were spread over four floors. The unadorned display areas included electric lighting and a sprinkler system. This photograph of c1900 shows a display of dining-room furniture. (Courtesy of Oliver Lebus)*

or stanchions of cruciform section carrying wrought-iron or steel floor joists (Fig 25). Brick party walls and floorboards were left bare, and the ceilings lined with matchboarding. The furniture was usually displayed by type, stacked closely together, sometimes with items suspended from the ceiling joists (Fig 26). The best quality goods were often displayed on the ground or first floors, and the bigger firms, such as C & R Light at 134–146 Curtain Road, had fully-furnished 'rooms' so that 'retailers could bring their friends to see such finished furnishings complete, even down to the books on the table' (Fig 27).

The upper floors were often used as stock rooms, for storing goods 'in the white' – unpolished and upholstered. The finishing would then take place in nearby workshops. Private rooms for the use of clients

Fig 26 *One of the many showrooms of Alfred Goslett & Co at 69–85 Tabernacle Street, pictured in 1911. Although the showroom has a carpet the interior is still otherwise plain.*

Fig 27 *The complete ensemble; a room furnished in a historical style, taken from the 1909 catalogue of Sadgrove and Co. (Geffrye Museum, London)*

and managers were sometimes provided; these might be quite grandly finished with high-quality wood and glass partitions. Offices for the clerks and salesmen were usually provided, as were drawing offices for the draughtsmen who worked on new designs and illustrations for catalogues. These were often located on the ground or first floor.

Despatch and delivery of goods was generally through loophole bays with taking-in doors and wall cranes on the front or side of the building, or alternatively through trapdoors in the pavement and basement hoists. Internal goods lifts, when they existed, were often hand operated, although by the 1890s the more prestigious premises had hydraulically or electrically powered lifts. Fire prevention was a significant issue because of the presence of workshops and flammable materials, yet fireproof construction in the form of brick or concrete jack arching was rare. Such disdain for fireproof construction was widespread in London's late-19th-century commercial buildings. In Shoreditch, as elsewhere, a degree of fire protection was obtained simply by separating areas with iron fire doors, and, at the turn of the 20th century, by the installation of sprinkler systems (Fig 28).

As a building type the showroom-warehouse was by no means unique to South Shoreditch or to the furniture trade. Similar examples of commercial warehouses for other trades can still be found elsewhere in London – in the City, Whitechapel, Clerkenwell and Southwark. The same generic building type was adapted to a wide range of uses in other cities and for other industries, including textile manufacturing and dealing in Manchester, jewellery in Birmingham, and footwear in Northamptonshire. In South Shoreditch, the particular importance of the commercial warehouse was as an interface between the spheres of production and consumption; the place in which an industry's goods were brought from factories or workshops, finished if necessary, and displayed before passing on to High Street stores and other retail outlets.

Fig 28 *The SCP furniture showrooms at 135–139 Curtain Road retains a turn-of-the-century sprinkler system. The building, dating from 1877, was erected for Saul Moss & Sons, wholesale furniture manufacturers, and was later used by another firm, Beresford and Hicks. Its continuing association with the furniture industry is now almost unique in the area.*

Workshops

Furniture manufacture encompassed a number of distinct processes.
First the timber had to be seasoned, cut and shaped. Then the
components had to be assembled and the items finished – decorated,
polished and, if necessary, upholstered. In the East End trade these
separate stages might take place in different locations involving
several businesses, or they might all occur under the roof of a single
manufacturer. However it was organised, manufacturing was likely to be
on a relatively modest scale (Fig 29). In the 1880s the typical unit size
in the East End was eight workers or fewer: a medium-sized firm would
employ 15 to 20 men, and only three or four businesses employed over
50. One exceptional firm, Harris Lebus, had almost 1,000 workers
and 45 staff by the 1890s, but this scale of operation was rare. Small
businesses were still the norm in the 1930s, when the authors of
The New Survey of London Life and Labour noted a large number of

Fig 29 *A group of three workshops, 8–10 New North
Place, dating from 1895. The interiors are restricted in
size as the buildings are quite shallow in depth, suitable
only for small-scale businesses.*

Fig 30 *This alley off Cheshire Street in Bethnal Green, 3–9 Hare Court, was built as weaver's housing around 1725. The presence of a barrow containing part-assembled drawers indicates that in 1928, when the photograph was taken, at least one of the residents was a cabinet maker. (© Crown copyright. NMR)*

two- to six-man concerns,[10] and in the 1950s the average unit size was eight to eleven. From the early 20th century the bigger firms tended to move away from Shoreditch to larger sites, many shifting further east to the Lea Valley, forming a concentration that was sometimes known as the 'outer' East London trade to differentiate it from its older heartland.

The extreme of small-scale manufacturing was the 'garret master', noted by social commentators such as Henry Mayhew in the 1850s and Ernest Aves in the 1880s. These were hand-to-mouth, one-person operations usually working within the home, producing only one or two items a week either to order or speculatively, to be hawked around the dealers and retailers. This class of maker was particularly associated with Bethnal Green, where the garret masters sometimes occupied tenement buildings and dwellings that had originally been developed for silk weavers (Fig 30). However, South Shoreditch also had its share of domestic working, such as Mrs Sturger, an upholsteress who was noted by one of the investigators for Booth's monumental survey of London life and labour as carrying on 'in a small way of business' from her parlour at 22 Curtain Road in the 1880s. It is difficult now to identify these types of premises as later developments have swept so many away.

More characteristic of South Shoreditch was the workshop proper, which existed in rich diversity by the end of the 19th century. The earliest form was probably the rear workshop, present on Old Street, Charlotte Road and Curtain Road by the early 19th century. Some wholesale manufacturers required extensive workshops, which might, if land was available, spread widely. Sites on the older thoroughfares such as Old Street, City Road and Curtain Road sometimes had long back plots that could be covered with workshops while presenting deceptively narrow frontages to the street (Fig 31). Rear workshops remained prevalent across the district until the latter part of the 20th century, subject to frequent replacement because of fire or poor construction.

It was also common for the front houses to be taken over for industrial purposes. For example 35 Scrutton Street, a mid-19th-century terrace house, functioned as cabinet works between the 1880s and 1960s. Now returned to domestic use, only the presence of a simple hoist on the upper storey hints at the building's previous history.

Fig 31 *The site of 346–348 Old Street was being used for furniture making in 1832. Over the following decades the rear yards and outbuildings were transformed into the dense mass of workshops depicted in this advertisement of 1886. John Barr & Sons occupied the premises from 1865 until the early 20th century, rebuilding both of the front showrooms between 1902 and 1904. (Permission British Library LD128)*

These conversions were often of the most basic kind, omitting taking-in doors or hoists so that furniture had to be moved between the floors through trapdoors. In the 1860s and 1870s there were a few purpose-built developments combining shops and dwellings with rear workshop accommodation. The most architecturally notable of these was the row at 91–101 Worship Street built in 1862–3 for the philanthropist Colonel Gillum to the designs of Philip Webb (Fig 32). More typical was the modest terrace at 7–15 New Inn Yard, a speculative development of the mid-1870s.

From the 1860s the construction of separate workshops as self-contained premises, rather than as adjuncts to other buildings, began in earnest. Some of these were speculative developments on an extensive scale, the largest being the dense manufacturing quarter

Fig 32 (opposite) *A row of six houses with shops and rear workshops at 91–101 Worship Street. Philip Webb's design of 1862–3 appears to be a conscious evocation of local vernacular building traditions and was not imitated by later buildings.*

around Phipp Street and Luke Street, rebuilt as island blocks of back-to-back workshops in the 1860s and 1870s (Figs 33 and 34). One of the most impressive developments was a terrace of 10 workshops at 65–83 Leonard Street, built between 1874 and 1877 (Fig 35). Such buildings were generally of three storeys with basements, and had functional elevations of brick piers, usually rising uninterrupted from the ground to a brick or stucco cornice, interspersed with windows or loophole bays with taking-in doors. The interiors were constructed simply, with wooden floors and stairs which were sometimes little more than ladders. Generally they were built without internal hoists, the lifting work being done by hand or by external wall cranes. The self-contained workshop reached its grandest form with 43–49 Charlotte Road, a row

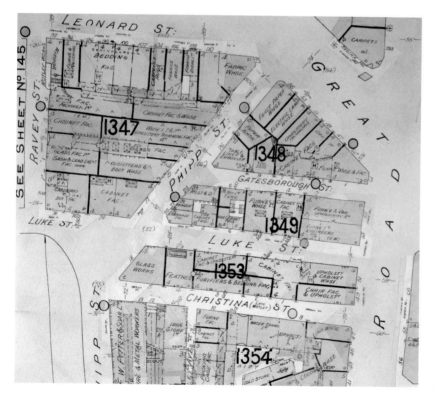

Fig 33 *The area around Phipp Street and Luke Street was redeveloped in the late-19th century as a dense concentration of workshops and warehouses. A Goad Insurance map, dating from 1922 with later amendments, shows the predominance of the furniture trade.*

Fig 34 *An island block, bounded by Christina Street, Curtain Road, Luke Street and Phipp Street, built between 1867 and 1871. The loophole bays and metal-framed windows indicate the industrial origins of the buildings but flats and restaurants now occupy what were once manufacturing spaces.*

Fig 35 *The impressive terrace of workshops, 65–83 Leonard Street was built between 1874 and 1877. Its impact derives partly from the great length of unified façade and the powerful rhythm of its closely spaced arcade of brick piers. Each property has a three-bay frontage, with windows flanking a loophole bay. The group retains a variety of iron or steel wall cranes of various dates.*

of seven four-storey buildings developed by John King Farlow between 1877 and 1881 (Fig 36). These had a higher level of embellishment than was the norm and, like the Leonard Street terrace, were built with integral one-storey back ranges. This was an efficient arrangement allowing for optimum lighting and access to both front and back for the delivery of materials and dispatch of goods. Because these buildings were provided with large shop windows on the ground floor, they could function equally as showroom-warehouses, and if machinery was installed, as factories.

In contrast to these prestigious developments were the more crudely built workshops which, in the last third of the 19th century, were shoehorned into the alleys and courts off the main roads. Surviving examples include Standard Place, off Rivington Street, and 5–6 Bowl Court, the remnants of a mass of buildings that were once crammed

Fig 36 *One of the most impressive workshop developments in the area, 43–49 Charlotte Street, was developed between 1877 and 1881. Furniture making and furnishing continued in these buildings until at least the 1950s.*

into this former yard between Shoreditch High Street and the viaduct of
the North London Railway (Fig 37).

Because of the modest size of many businesses, multiple occupation
of workshops was commonplace. When different types of firms shared
the same premises a 'hand-in-hand' system was able to develop, as
articles of furniture passed from one business to another, completing
each stage of the production process in turn. Within such multi-
tenanted workshops space could be let by the floor or the room, and the
turnover of occupants was generally very rapid.

The important role of small-scale operations within the trade was
probably a factor in the resurgence of workshop building in the 1890s
and 1900s. Many of these new buildings were modest structures, like
the two rows built by the furniture manufacturer William Ratcliffe at
16–26 and 17–29 Rivington Street in 1897, constructed on the same
scale as the terrace houses that they replaced (Fig 38). These functional
brick workshops were sometimes provided with simple beam hoists and

Fig 37 *A back-alley workshop, probably dating from
the 1870s, in Bowl Court off Shoreditch High Street.
The arches of the adjoining railway viaduct were also
used as workshops and timber stores.*

Fig 38 *An industrial terrace of six workshops, 16–26 Rivington Street, built in 1897. Utilitarian in appearance, they were apparently constructed with flat roofs possibly to allow for additional storeys.*

loading doors. Inside were wooden floors, usually carried on steel joists, and, in some instances, rear lean-tos with skylights providing additional ground-floor workspace.

In Bethnal Green a much larger speculative development by Henry and Charles Winkley in 1898–1903 combined residential buildings with factories and workshops. Laid out between Teesdale Street and Temple Street, the workshops were in separate blocks of two or three storeys placed in narrow yards between the ranges of dwellings (Fig 39). Under construction at the same time were the first municipally provided workshops, part of the London County Council's pioneering Boundary Street Estate, erected between 1894 and 1900 just to the east of Shoreditch High Street. Four blocks of workshops were constructed to replace the workrooms and backyard workshops that were swept away for the slum clearance scheme; three – Cleeve, Sunbury and Marlow workshops – still survive (Fig 40). After the Second World War, when large areas of the East End were earmarked for comprehensive development, London County Council sought to sustain the area's characteristic form of manufacturing through the

Fig 39 (opposite) *The interior of an upholstery workshop in Bethnal Green in 2001. Part of an extraordinary development by Henry and Charles Winkley, built between 1898 and 1903, that combined dwellings, shops, factories and workshops.*

Fig 40 *The three surviving workshops of the LCC Boundary Street Estate, built between 1894 and 1900: Cleeve Workshops (top); Marlow Workshops (middle); Sunbury Workshop (bottom). The two-storey blocks are divided into units of four with a central taking-in door serving the upper pair. Extra light is provided by roof lights, to the front on the Marlow block and at the rear on the Sunbury buildings. These well-built workshops have remained in demand, used over the years by many different small firms from all branches of the furniture trade.*

construction of 'flatted factories'. Several, including the four-storey blocks at Long Street off Hackney Road, erected in 1959 (Fig 41), were built with the furniture industry in mind.

Many firms, however, continued to occupy older premises. Until the trade collapsed in the 1980s South Shoreditch, Hoxton and Bethnal Green had many examples of the 'rambling workshops' evoked by John Betjeman in his autobiographical poem *Summoned by Bells*, fondly recalling the family cabinet-maker's shop in Pentonville.[11]

Fig 41 *Part of the complex of flatted factories on Long Street, built by the London County Council in 1959. The concrete-framed blocks were provided with generously sized lifts able to take uncut sheets of plywood.*

Small factories

As the extensive use of powered machinery came relatively late, the furniture industry was slow to adopt factory-based manufacturing. From the 1870s the greater availability of woodworking machinery encouraged the appearance of what in South Shoreditch were termed 'factories', although many of these were simply workshops into which steam or gas-powered machinery had been installed.

East End furniture factories were usually divided into chair and cabinet departments with separate workshops for the upholsterers and polishers, while the woodworking machinery was usually grouped together, usually on the ground floor or in the basement. This arrangement, well established by the 1880s, was to change little over the following century (Fig 42). Because demand fluctuated, space in the machine shops was sometimes rented to self-employed machinists. Power was initially supplied by gas or steam engines, housed in separate buildings or, if this was not possible, in the basement (Fig 43). The machinery was driven by belts attached to shafts and later by electric

Fig 42 *A basement machine shop at 16 Provost Street with Mr Brian Laye operating a table saw. Light from the ground-floor windows is able to reach the basement by canting or splaying the ceiling upwards before it meets the front wall. This feature can be found in manufacturing buildings across the district.*

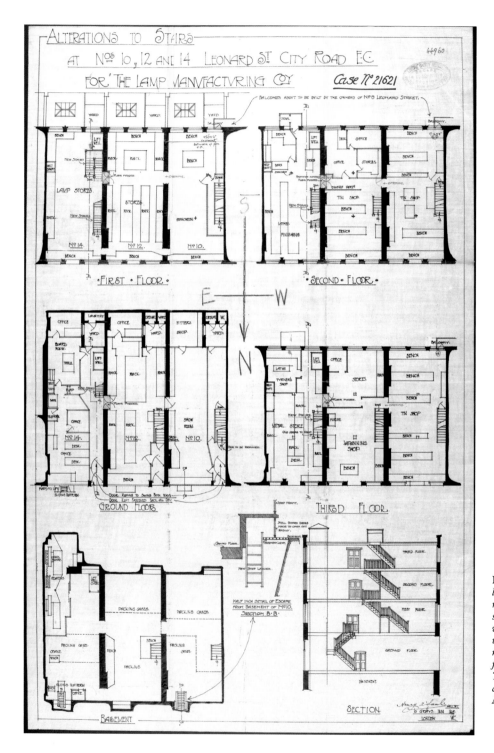

Fig 43 *10–14 Leonard Street typifies the layout of a workshop or small factory. Largely rebuilt in 1883, the three buildings were in single occupation in 1907 when these plans were drawn. They had workrooms on the upper floors containing benches and some machinery, operated by line shafting powered from a gas engine in the basement of No. 14. The ground floor housed a modest showroom and offices. (Corporation of London, London Metropolitan Archives)*

Fig 44 *The 'machine shop' in the factory of E Kahn and Co Ltd in Gough Street, Holborn in 1905.*

motors. For some firms the machine shop might contain little more than a few circular saws and band-saws in the corner of a workshop (Fig 44).

The larger establishments sometimes had more extensive machine shops, often known as 'steam cabinet works'. One example was to be found in the premises of W Walker and Sons on Bunhill Row, which in 1883 contained front showrooms and rear four-storey workshops around a covered yard spanned by bridges (Fig 45). The steam-powered machinery for cutting and shaping the wood was on the ground floor, while the cabinet makers, polishers and upholsterers occupied workshops on the upper floors. A hand lift in the centre of the yard was used to move goods between floors.

In the 1890s more advanced furniture factories began to be built in London and in other manufacturing centres such as Manchester and Glasgow. The significant innovation of such factories was to introduce

Fig 45 *The steam cabinet works of William Walker and Sons, depicted on a trade card of the 1880s. The machinery was located on the ground floor beneath the workshops, while the yard was used as a packing space and wood store. (Geffrye Museum, London)*

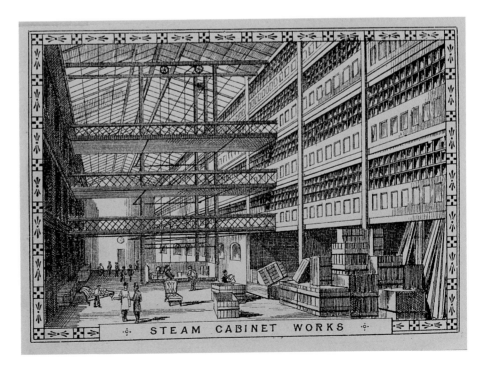

STEAM CABINET WORKS

flow-line production, eradicating 'the hauling up and down and lifting about, generally associated with the cabinet making works'.[12] In the East End, where land was scarce and expensive, it was only possible to build multi-storey factories of a medium size, but further out sprawling single-storey sites could be erected, such as Harris Lebus's Finsbury Works in Tottenham in 1900–1 (Fig 46).

Fig 46 *An aerial view of Lebus's vast Finsbury Works, Tottenham, mostly of one storey with sawtooth roofs. The factory opened in 1901 and was extended in the 1930s. The image, taken from a 1930s trade catalogue, also includes a view of the main showroom on Tabernacle Street in the right-hand corner. (Geffrye Museum, London)*

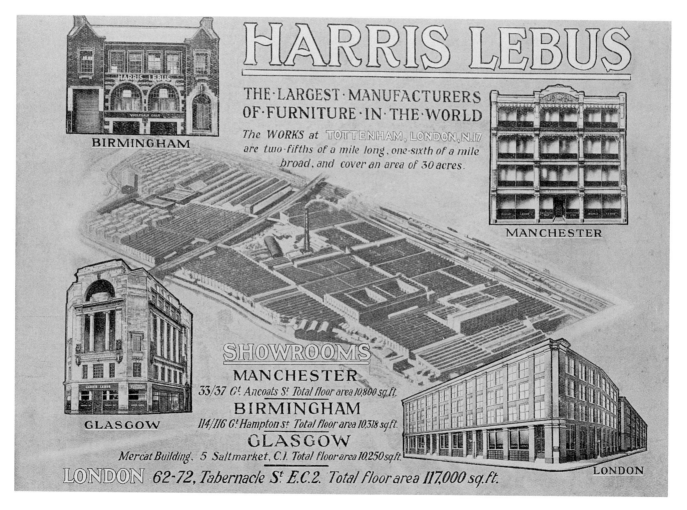

Fig 47 *The assembly and finishing shop in the Beresford and Hicks factory in Hemsworth Street, Hoxton in 1951. The firm remained loyal to its East End roots and continued to manufacture a wide range of furniture from this site between the 1930s and the 1960s. (Hackney Archives Department)*

Fig 48 *Newly finished furniture, some still 'in the white', and older pieces in for repair in the factory of J Wernick (Furniture) Ltd, 16 Provost Street, Hoxton in 2003. The building dates from around 1900.*

One of the first examples of this new approach was William Angus's four-storey 'model factory' on Stour Road in Old Ford, built in 1899 to produce roll-top desks. The wooden components that made up the desks were imported precut from the United States and transported along the Regent's Canal to the factory. The manufacturing process then flowed upwards through the building, culminating in the polishing department on the top storey. The finished items were then lowered back down for packing and delivery.

Angus was an American manufacturer, keen to introduce new American production methods into the British trade. Fear of losing ground to US competitors led the Shoreditch firm C & R Light to set up a bedroom-suite factory at 82 Great Eastern Street in 1897–8, deploying the latest machinery and, so they claimed, a more efficient production process. Because only one class of goods – bedroom furniture or roll-top desks – was manufactured in these buildings, the scope for something nearer to mass production was increased.

More typical of the East End trade was the four-storey factory built for Beresford and Hicks in Hemsworth Street, Hoxton, in 1930 (Fig 47). Here the firm manufactured a wide range of furniture, including bespoke items, reproduction pieces and standard lines, on a small scale and in a more traditionally organised way. The mill shop on the ground floor supplied the timber for both regular production and special orders. Each article was assembled by one man, and there was no mechanical handling of the furniture between the various stages of manufacture. Chair making was an entirely separate department, and the upholstering took place above the showrooms at 135–139 Curtain Road.

One innovation of the 1930s was the spray shop, replacing the more traditional method of French polishing. Another change in the inter-war years was the rise of separate 'trade mills' to prepare the timber. This left some factories simply as places of assembly and finishing, including that of J Wernick, 16 Provost Street, which was still operating in this way in 2003 (Fig 48).

The associated trades, timber yards and commercial saw-mills

The highly developed network of suppliers to the East End furniture trade encompassed diverse activities, including cabinet ironmongers, upholstery and trimmings wholesalers, toolmakers, woodworking machinery suppliers, and specialist cart and van builders to serve the industry's transportation needs. Many of these businesses required the same type of facilities as the furniture trade, competing with it for the showroom-warehouses and manufacturing facilities of the district, and underscoring the adaptability of the building types. In 1898, for example, C W Waters, varnish makers, had a showroom at 72 Great Eastern Street, an adjoining warehouse on Garden Walk, and a factory in Bateman's Row. From these various premises the firm manufactured and supplied all manner of glues, colours, varnishes, stains, gums and lacquers to the trade.

After the furniture wholesalers began to decline in importance and the larger manufacturers began to move away from Shoreditch in the early 20th century, the suppliers became an increasing presence in the district. Firms such as Amos Oakden & Sons and W A Hudson, both cabinet ironmongers, eventually grew into vast concerns. Oakden's premises at 86–90 Curtain Road became something of a local landmark, occupying a prominent corner site (Figs 24 and 49), while Hudson's, which started manufacturing curtain poles on New Inn Broadway in 1890, encompassed 117–119 Curtain Road and 51–60 Charlotte Road (Figs 10 and 50).

For the suppliers of the industry's most essential raw material, timber, a slightly different set of requirements pertained. Most timber was imported, and there were large storage facilities at the docks. From the mid-19th century almost all sawing was done in steam-powered factory mills, many located on the Regent's Canal just to the north of Shoreditch. The seasoning and storage of cut timber required a range of facilities including drying sheds and timber platforms or stages as well as machine shops, office accommodation and, for the storage and display of veneers, a showroom and warehouse. Such

Showing Premises situated at Junction of Curtain Road and Gt. Eastern Street, Shoreditch, London, E.C.2.

The Tablet on this building indicates that this was the site of the Priory of St. John the Baptist, Holywell, and also that from 1577 to 1598 there stood here the first London theatre.

Fig 49 *The firm of Amos Oakden and Sons was an early occupant of 86–90 Curtain Road, present from the 1890s. By the 1930s the firm had taken over the entire block. Its position, at the junction of Curtain Road and Great Eastern Street, put it right at the heart of the furniture-making district. (Geffrye Museum, London)*

premises were usually sited within the district so as to be near to the manufacturers (Fig 51).

One site on the corner of Curtain Road and Rivington Street was already an extensive timber yard by 1832. In about 1850 it was acquired by James Latham, the founder of what has now become a nationally important business. A saw-mill and separate departments for veneers and mouldings were added before much of the site was destroyed by fire in 1892. The rebuilt premises were then used for hardwood and veneer storage until the firm moved away in 1940. One of the characteristic building types of such yards was the seasoning shed, usually built with brick walls and a flat roof for storing timber, and with distinctive vertical openings to the sides to allow air to circulate around the cut wood stacked inside. The three-storey shed with a 20ft-high ground floor that stood in John Burton and Son's yard at 32 Rivington Street was probably the largest example of this type in the district. Two much altered examples at 74 Rivington Street and at the rear of 124 Curtain Road survive from Latham's yard (Figs 52 and 53).

Fig 50 *Loading doors at the rear of 55 Charlotte Road, the painted signage of the building's former occupant still prominent. Until the 1980s W A Hudson continued to occupy a site spread over many properties, the full extent of which can be seen in Fig 10.*

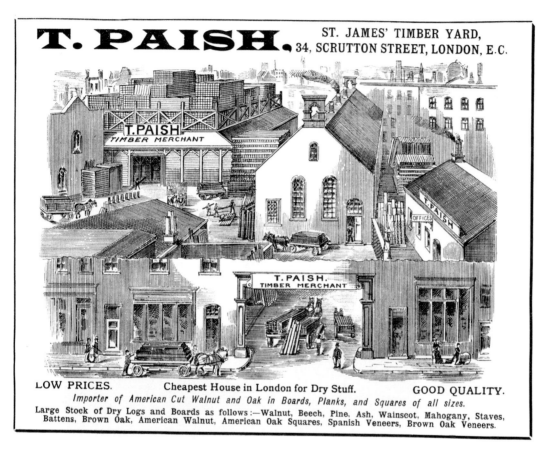

Fig 51 *A view of Paish's timber yard behind the cut-away front premises on Scrutton Street showing the sawmill, timber stores and offices. The street buildings probably contained a showroom for veneers. Taken from an advert in the* Cabinet Maker *in 1890.*
(Per.1753.c.4, © Bodleian Library, University of Oxford)

Fig 52 (opposite above) *One of two surviving seasoning sheds, part of the former timber yard of James Latham. This example, at the rear of 124 Curtain Road, was probably built in 1892. Its upper openings are now filled with windows and the building converted to a bar.*

Fig 53 (opposite) *Another former seasoning shed, 74 Rivington Street, built for James Latham in 1898–9. Rather more grandly treated than the other shed, perhaps because it fronts onto the street, the building has also been converted and its elongated openings glazed.*

Some of the timber dealers, like Barnett Moss at 2 Hoxton Street, rented out facilities to turners, moulders and other small makers. Moss supplied space in the mill, the power and, unless the maker bought his own machinery, the lathes. This type of subletting was common, much of it taking place in what were often described as 'commercial saw-mills'. The self-employed machinists who used these mills supplied the small amounts of worked timber required by firms that were making up only a few items of furniture per week. These mills were often in adapted buildings or back-yard workshops such as at 92–94 Curtain Road (Fig 54). This row of three ordinary shops and dwellings had a two-storey saw-mill and timber store at the rear, the earliest part of which probably dates back to 1846, when a steam engine was installed there. Operating as a saw-mill and steam-turning works throughout the second half of the 19th century (Fig 55), these buildings continued as a store and shop for the veneer merchants Crispins throughout the 20th century.

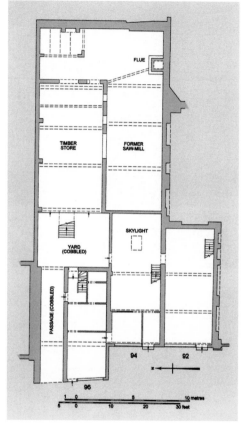

Fig 54 *A ground-floor plan of 92–96 Curtain Road in 2002, before the demolition of the rear buildings, a former saw-mill and timber store.*

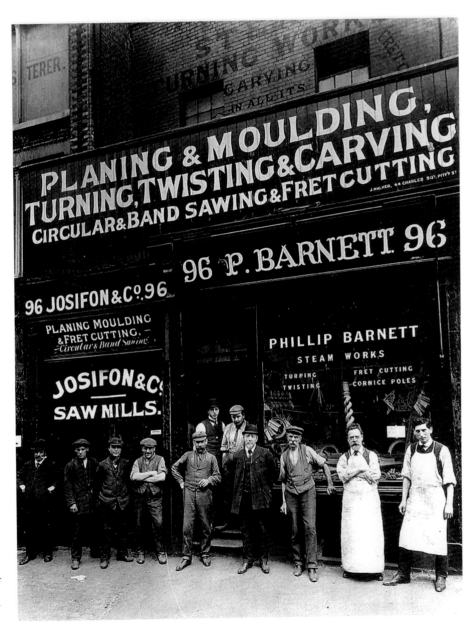

Fig 55 *Phillip Barnett and his staff in front of 96 Curtain Road in c1900. A succession of wood turners occupied these premises during the second half of the 19th century. (Hackney Archives Department)*

'What is left of furniture making in the East End is only a shadow of what was once one of London's most thriving and important manufacturing industries.'

Kirkham *et al*, *Furnishing the World*, 1987

5
POSTSCRIPT: THE END OF THE FURNITURE TRADE

The Second World War brought great disruption to the East End furniture trade. Many firms moved into aircraft manufacture, and some premises were lost to bomb damage. When the trade revived what remained was its more traditional sector, specialising in high-quality reproduction furniture, as the mass production of cheaper goods was taken over by the larger manufacturers based in the Lea Valley and elsewhere. By 1980 the English furniture industry was in crisis, unable to compete with cheaper imports. The modest levels of productivity and old-fashioned premises of the East End manufacturers made them particularly vulnerable, and as fewer young people chose to enter the trade the industry here collapsed. By the end of the 20th century only a handful of firms remained (Fig 56), although a connection has endured through the designer-makers who continue to use some of the workshops of the district. Many of these are graduates of the London College of Furniture, based in Whitechapel, which has its origins in a Technical School for the furniture industry in Pitfield Street, Hoxton, set up by the London County Council around 1899. Another connection exists in the Geffrye Museum in Kingsland Road, established in 1912–13 as a museum of woodwork and furniture in a group of former almshouses.

The economic revival of South Shoreditch has partly come about through the needs of the financial services industry spilling out from the City of London, resulting in some massive glossy office developments in the area south of Worship Street. Much more sympathetic to the historic fabric of the area have been the small media, design and arts based companies of the 'cultural industries' (Fig 57). Such businesses have found the modest scale and relatively simple form of the area's buildings well suited to their need, as well as supplying character and

Fig 56 *Detail of the exterior of 16 Provost Street. One of the few functioning furniture factories when photographed in 2003, the building was converted into flats in 2006.*

historical 'authenticity'. These industries present some parallels with the older trades of the district, thriving on close proximity, taking 'the same comfort from agglomeration – face-to-face contact between innovators, labour market and commissioning networks – that had kept the furniture … industries flourishing in the same spaces sixty years before'.[13] As well as perpetuating the intimate commercial character of South Shoreditch, this has enabled the distinctive qualities of its urban townscape to survive.

Fig 57 *The darkrooms and work areas of Rapid Eye, a company supplying photographic services, at 79 Leonard Street. The firm occupies a former furniture workshop of the 1870s.*

Painted signage in French Place.

6

PLANNING AND CONSERVATION ISSUES

Ray Rogers

Introduction

Following the demise of the furniture trade in the early 1980s, South Shoreditch initially went through a period of decline, with many buildings left vacant and underused. Then the process of adaptation began. The buildings of the furniture trade became popular with artists, the relatively cheap and large open spaces within them making perfect studios. Later, galleries, architects' offices and design studios were established, and proximity to the expanding City made the area ideal for small media and information-technology companies servicing the financial sector. At the same time the buildings and the location of the South Shoreditch and Hoxton areas attracted the new cultural phenomenon of late-night bars and clubs, originally encouraged in the attempt to build a 24-hour economy. The transformation of the area was boosted in the mid-1980s with the completion of the first phases of the nearby Broadgate area, a large-scale office development that attracted major financial and professional organisations (Fig 59).

By the mid-1990s South Shoreditch was fully established as a busy mixed economy, containing a significant part of Hackney's employment base, and with significant commercial and cultural sectors. It has a burgeoning night time economy and a growing residential population.

The area lies in the shadow of the City of London, one of the world's great financial centres and the source of much of the nation's wealth. The City's success over the last two decades has led to an immense demand for new commercial space, partly satisfied by more intensive development within the traditional trading core, but also by expansion into the fringe areas of Clerkenwell, South Shoreditch and Spitalfields. Continuing expansion has led to a range of potential conflicts between different uses and differing perceptions of the area, and much attention has recently been directed to resolving these competing issues.

Fig 58 *The heart of South Shoreditch, the junction of Great Eastern Street and Curtain Road, in 2005. The imposing corner building with the battlemented roofline and ground-floor porch, 40–42 Great Eastern Street, is amongst the best of the speculative developments that followed the formation of the new road in 1872–6.*

Policy initiatives

The pressures for change in the City fringe are being addressed in current and emerging policies of the Greater London Authority (GLA) and the London boroughs. The London Plan, the strategic planning framework for London published in 2004, identifies the need for a number of sub-regional development frameworks and opportunity area frameworks to assist the boroughs in achieving a sustainable and prosperous future. Administratively, South Shoreditch lies mainly within the borough of Hackney, with its outer edges falling within Tower Hamlets to the east and Islington to the west. It forms part of the City Fringe Opportunity Area Framework prepared by the Mayor in partnership with the three boroughs and the City Corporation.

Within the policy framework set by the London Plan, Hackney is revising its Unitary Development Plan and replacing it with the new style Local Development Framework (LDF). The LDF includes a Supplementary Planning Document (SPD) for South Shoreditch, which provides supplementary guidance to assist in the determination of planning applications in the area.

Threats to the area

Since the early 1990s South Shoreditch has seen a massive increase in economic activity which, whilst bringing in much needed investment, has put the special character of the area and its buildings under threat. The current pressures on the area include site assembly for large-scale office development; piecemeal demolition and infill development, and unsympathetic additions and alterations to existing buildings. This has led to a slow but incremental loss of character. It is clear that the existing planning and conservation powers are insufficient to guide and control future development effectively without further erosion and loss of the area's special qualities.

The issue of how economic development within the City fringe can be married to continued enjoyment of the area's historic character was

Fig 59 *The encroaching City: a view southwards along Curtain Road. The scale of recent office developments is significantly larger than even the post-war rebuilding of the 1950s and 1960s.*

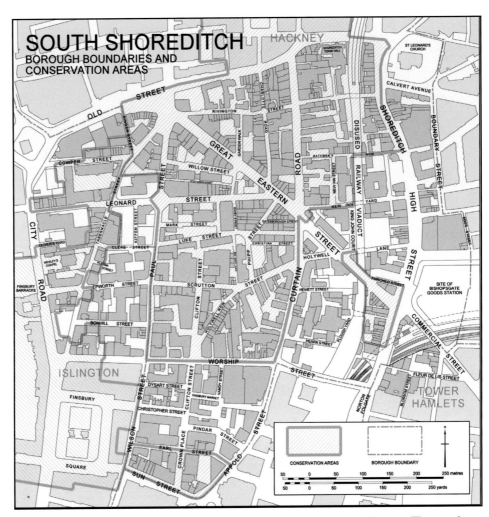

Fig 60 *Map of South Shoreditch showing the borough boundaries and the conservation areas. The area of the English Heritage study is indicated by the dark grey shading.*

Fig 61 *A workshop still in industrial use, 43–47 Rivington Street, occupied by Framers Buttons & Trimming Suppliers. The film crew operating in the street is now perhaps more typical of the South Shoreditch economy.*

addressed in 2003, when Hackney Council, English Heritage and the GLA jointly commissioned a study of South Shoreditch from Urban Practitioners and Alan Baxter Associates. The objective of the study was to inform decision making in a number of key areas, including local development, growth and regeneration, and transport and public realm improvements. The historic environment was acknowledged to be an important consideration in all these areas, and the study's recommendations have informed the SPD.

Character of the area

The key to success in South Shoreditch lies in solutions which allow the local economy to grow whilst also protecting the area's strong individual qualities. Good decision making depends on a thorough understanding of present character and what is of value in the historic environment. English Heritage's own Architectural Investigation report has provided this understanding for South Shoreditch, and has highlighted a number of key historic attributes: a dense network of streets, some ancient, many more recent; a close grain, which results from the individual development of relatively small plots; and a concentration of late-19th- and early-20th-century commercial buildings, built mainly to support the needs of the furniture trade. Most of these buildings are architecturally modest, but collectively they are of historic interest and give strong identity to the area (Fig 61).

The particular character of South Shoreditch was recognised as long ago as 1986, when the Hackney Society published an important study of its buildings. The Society called for the designation of a Conservation Area to provide protection against undesirable changes brought about by the upturn in the area's fortunes following the redevelopment at Broadgate. Subsequently, Hackney Council designated three conservation areas covering much of the study area (Fig 60), and also published urban design guidance for the area.

Character areas

As part of the Local Planning Framework process, South Shoreditch has been subdivided into three distinct 'character areas': the Shoreditch Triangle, the Leonard Circus area and the Edge of City area (Fig 62). Character areas are a helpful way of understanding conservation areas that contain development from more than one period. In South Shoreditch, for example, areas of Georgian, Victorian and later development, combined with industrial and commercial activities, have created discernible 'sub areas' of relatively consistent character.

The Shoreditch Triangle, bounded by Great Eastern Street and Old Street, is the heart of Shoreditch, with its intimate street pattern and dense cluster of historic buildings. Today it has a wealth of cultural uses such as galleries, arts and crafts showrooms, media studios and workshops. The numerous bars and clubs make the area a popular evening destination, enhanced by its strong historic character. Within the Triangle, Charlotte Road, lined with historic commercial buildings, is one of the architectural highlights of South Shoreditch (Fig 63).

The Leonard Circus area, focused on Paul Street, Scrutton Street and Leonard Street, lies between Great Eastern Street and Worship Street, and illustrates the overlaying of earlier Georgian townscape by Victorian development, with many fine survivors of the buildings of the furniture and printing industries. The scale of most of the area's buildings is modest, and the complex historic street pattern survives largely intact. The damage that can be done to the character of an area is evident in some of the more recent development of variable quality, but despite some insensitive intrusions the area retains its identity.

The Edge of City areas, south of Worship Street and east of Curtain Road around Hearn Street, are transition zones between the City and South Shoreditch proper, occupying a strategically important location linking the area to Finsbury Square and Broadgate, as well as connecting the City with a potential new development area at Bishopsgate. The eastern part of this area is dominated by gap sites ready for redevelopment, and this creates an important opportunity for the extension of the City towards the Bishopsgate Goodsyard site,

Fig 62 *Map showing the three character areas from the South Shoreditch Supplementary Planning Document. (© Crown copyright. All rights reserved. LB Hackney LA08638X (2003))*

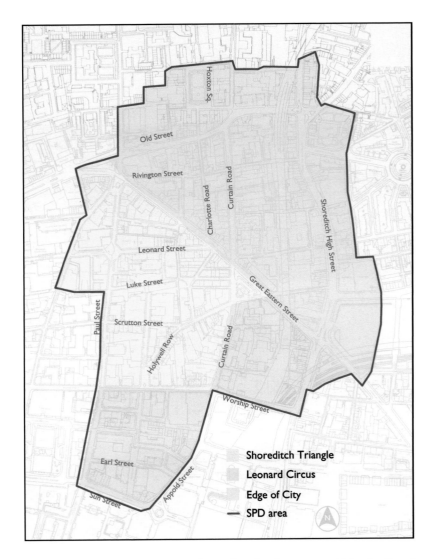

helping to relieve the pressure for major development within the South Shoreditch conservation area. The southern area, south of Worship Street, lies in the shadow of the expanding City, but still retains its fine grain and many early commercial buildings.

The buildings of the area

As of late 2005 there are 35 listed buildings in the South Shoreditch study area, 28 in Hackney and 7 in Islington. Some of these are prominent public buildings, like Shoreditch Town Hall, Wesley's Chapel and St Leonard's Church. Few of the buildings of the furniture and associated trades meet the stringent criteria for listing, although English Heritage's research has identified a number of candidates for consideration. Listed or not, however, many of the buildings identified in the English Heritage Architectural Investigation report are of intrinsic architectural merit, have local significance, and are excellent examples of Victorian and early 20th-century design. There are also many buildings of townscape merit that contribute to the overall quality of the area, and act as a setting for the furniture trade showpieces. It is this combination that gives the best and most characteristic parts of South Shoreditch special character as an industrial and commercial quarter of considerable historic interest. As we have seen, the furniture trade developed its own distinctive building types, and the warehouse-showroom, five or six storeys high, remains a characteristic feature of South Shoreditch, especially along the main thoroughfares of Great Eastern Street, Curtain Road and Tabernacle Street. Good examples of workshops also survive in Charlotte Road, Rivington Street and the roads around Luke Street.

Conservation policies

Many of the buildings of South Shoreditch are adaptable for a wide range of uses, and it is this very mix that contributes so much to the vital character of the area. The type and scale of new development can, however, have a major impact on this character. The protection of plot patterns and resistance to the amalgamation of sites are key ways of protecting the grain of the historic townscape. There are relatively few sites within the conservation area large enough to accommodate single-use new office buildings, though there are some – for example at the junctions of Great Eastern Street and Curtain Road and of

Fig 63 *The former showroom of E Kahn & Co, furniture manufacturers, at 18–22 Charlotte Road, now the gallery of the Prince of Wales Foundation. It is glimpsed through the entrance to Mill Court at 55 Charlotte Road, which still retains its painted signage.*

Leonard Street and Paul Street – where the redevelopment of post-war office blocks would provide an opportunity to repair the townscape by recreating a street frontage with buildings of more sympathetic scale.

A great deal of piecemeal alteration has taken place, often to buildings of historic or architectural interest. This has included the replacement of original ground-floor elevations and the construction of roof extensions and other structures at roof level. Changes to windows and fenestration pattern can have a very damaging impact on the architectural integrity and character of a building.

A new approach to controlling alterations is needed, and this is being addressed in framing new conservation policies. The South Shoreditch SPD provides detailed guidance for conservation and design issues within the SPD boundary, covering the following policy areas:

- Detailed planning applications and design statements
- Protection of plot patterns
- Unlisted buildings of intrinsic interest
- Demolition and new development
- Alterations and extensions to buildings of intrinsic interest
- Roof extensions and structures on roofs
- Character of new development
- Floorscapes
- Shop fronts.

The policy guidance includes requirements for detailed planning applications to be accompanied by a design statement and views analysis for all significant planning applications within the SPD area; the protection of plot patterns; detailed criteria for new development relating to design quality, including materials, scale and relationship to context; and a range of urban design and townscape principles, including building heights and local views, the preservation of the historic street layout and urban form, together with the retention of surviving historic floorscapes and shop fronts.

As part of this approach the Council plans to review the boundaries of the South Shoreditch and Shoreditch High Street

Conservation Areas, and to prepare a detailed conservation area appraisal for each area. An Article 4 direction will be considered in respect of unlisted buildings of intrinsic interest located within the Conservation Areas.

Permission for alterations and extensions to buildings of intrinsic merit, as identified by the detailed study, will only be granted for schemes that reinstate lost or missing features of architectural or historic interest, including doors, shop or showroom fronts, and decorative details and cornices. In this way it is hoped that lost architectural detail will gradually be replaced. Roof extensions will not be permitted where the proposal would result in the loss of a historic roof form, harm the architectural integrity or proportions of a building or group of buildings, harm a significant view, or reduce the visual interest of the varied skyline – for example where a building has features that were meant to be silhouetted against the sky. This still leaves ample opportunities for the restoration and intensification of buildings within the conservation area by means of well-designed alterations and extensions to existing buildings (Fig 64).

Conclusion

South Shoreditch must inevitably change. It is essential that this change is managed in a sensitive way to allow – and indeed encourage – economic activity, at the same time protecting the architectural legacy that makes the area so attractive. The key to achieving this balance lies in a clear policy framework that encourages high-quality, large-scale development in the edge of city areas, whilst ensuring that development within conservation areas reflects the prevailing scale, character and form of the nationally important architectural legacy of the furniture trade.

The historic environment plays a significant part in enhancing the quality of people's lives. The model presented in South Shoreditch, where the assessment of character and significance has informed economic and conservation policy, can be applied elsewhere in the City fringe to help ensure that these areas retain the essential character that makes them such attractive places in which to live and work.

References

1 White, J 2002 *London in the Twentieth Century*. London: Viking

2 Schwarz, L D 1992 *London in the Age of Industrialisation*. Cambridge: Cambrige University Press

3 Hall, P 'Industrial London: a general view' *in* Coppock, J T and Prince, H 1964 *Greater London*. London: Faber

4 *Cabinet and Upholstery Advertiser*, 29 September 1877, 7

5 Booth, C 1889 *Life and Labour of the People*, vol 1. London: Williams & Norgate

6 *Cabinet Maker*, February 1890, **x**, 216

7 Aves, E 'The furniture trade' *in* Booth, C 1889 *op cit*, 1, 315

8 Anon, 'Centres of the furniture industry: the East End of London'. *The Woodworker* 1929, **xxxiii**, 221

9 *Cabinet Maker* April 1883, **iii**, 186

10 London School of Economics 1931 *The New Survey of London Life and Labour*, vol 2: London Industries. London: King & Sons

11 Betjeman, J 1960 *Summoned by Bells*. London: Murray

12 *Cabinet Maker and Art Furnisher*, November 1899, **iii**, 136

13 White, J *op cit*, 214

Fig 64 *The furniture showrooms of SCP, on the first floor of 135–139 Curtain Road. The well-handled refurbishment of the building in 2004–5, and the sympathetic use of the ground and first floors as furniture showrooms, has ensured the survival of many of its historic features.*

Further reading

Barnwell, P S, Palmer, M and Airs, M 2004 *The Vernacular Workshop from Craft to Industry, 1400–1900.* York: Council for British Archaeology

Draper, T and Smith, J 2004 *An industrial suburb: the commercial buildings of South Shoreditch 1850–1980.* (English Heritage Architectural Investigation Report B/018). London: English Heritage

Edwards, C 1993 *Victorian Furniture Technology and Design.* Manchester: Manchester University Press

Hackney Society 1986 *South Shoreditch Historical and Industrial Buildings.* London: Hackney Society

Joy, E T 1977 *English Furniture 1800–1851.* London: Sotheby Parke Bernet

Kirkham, P, Mace, R and Porter, J 1987 *Furnishing the World: The East London Furniture Trade 1830–1980.* London: Journeyman

Massil, W I 1997 *Immigrant Furniture Workers in London 1881–1939 and the Jewish Contribution to the Furniture Trade.* London: Jewish Museum

Oliver, J L 1961 'The East London furniture industry', *East London Papers*, vol 4, **2**, 88–101

Vaughan, A 1984 *The Vaughans, East End Furniture Makers: Three Hundred Years of a London Family.* London: privately published

Other titles in this series

The Birmingham Jewellery Quarter: An introduction and guide. John Cattell and Bob Hawkins, 2000. Product code 50204, ISBN 1850747776

'One Great Workshop': The buildings of the Sheffield metal trades. Nicola Wray, Bob Hawkins and Colum Giles, 2001. Product code 50214, ISBN 1873592663

Manchester: The Warehouse Legacy – An introduction and guide. Simon Taylor, Malcolm Cooper and P S Barnwell, 2002. Product code 50668, ISBN 1873592671

Newcastle's Grainger Town: An urban renaissance. Fiona Cullen and David Lovie, 2003. Product code 50811, ISBN 1873592779

Gateshead: Architecture in a changing English urban landscape. Simon Taylor and David Lovie, 2004. Product code 52000, ISBN 1873592760

Storehouses of Empire: Liverpool's historic warehouses. Colum Giles and Bob Hawkins, 2004. Product code 50920, ISBN 1873592809

Built to Last? The buildings of the Northamptonshire boot and shoe industry. Kathryn A Morrison with Ann Bond, 2004. Product code 50921, ISBN 1873592795

Bridport and West Bay: The buildings of the flax and hemp industry. Mike Williams, 2006. Product code 51167, ISBN-10 1873592868, ISBN-13 9781873592861

£7.99 each (plus postage and packing)

To order
Tel: EH Sales 01761 452966
Email: ehsales@gillards.com

Online bookshop: www.english-heritage-books.org.uk

Cover illustrations

Front cover   55 Charlotte Road, occupied by W A Hudson Ltd until the 1980s.

Inside front cover   A basement machine shop at 16 Provost Street.

Back cover   Details from an advertisement for B Cohen & Sons Ltd showing how its premises in Curtain Road were 'in the heart of the furniture industry'. (Geffrye Museum, London)

South Shoreditch and its environs